Python Lambda Functions

Elevating Your Functional Programming

Table of Contents

Chapter 1. Introduction

Welcome to this comprehensive Special Report on Python Lambda Functions: Elevating Your Functional Programming. This in-depth exploration aims to guide you step-by-step through the intricacies of Python's most powerful, if elusive, feature - Lambda Functions. This isn't some arcane or intricate terminology beyond the realms of mere mortals; instead, it's a practical and potent tool for effective and efficient coding. Ready to demystify Lambda Functions and witness how they can streamline your coding process while reducing redundancy? Uncover the transformative potential of Lambda Functions, irrespective of whether you're a seasoned programmer or starting your Python journey. This Special Report wraps up everything you need in an easy-to-understand, down-to-earth style. So, strap in for an enriching ride towards elevating your functional programming skills onto the next level.

Chapter 2. Demystifying Functional Programming: A Brief Introduction

Functional programming is a programming paradigm—a way of conceptualizing software development based around the process of functions. Many of us are familiar with the imperative programming paradigm, which emphasizes state and the changing state; that is, you focus on describing how something should happen.

Functional programming (FP), on the other hand, emphasizes operations as mathematical functions, avoiding changing state and mutable data. To better understand functional programming, let's dive into its key principles and distinctions.

2.1. Principles of Functional Programming

The approach towards programming taken by functional programming is significantly different from traditional imperative or procedural programming. A Function in this paradigm is more akin to a mathematical function that takes some input, performs computations on it, and returns some output. There are three primary principles of functional programming:

1. Pure Functions: A function is said to be pure if it always produces the same results given the same inputs. These functions have no side effects (i.e., they do not modify any arguments or global variables or print to the console or write to a file, etc.).

2. Immutability: In functional programming, once a data structure (like a list or dictionary) is created, it cannot be changed. Any operation that seems to modify the data structure instead creates

a new version that incorporates the requested changes.

3. High-Level Functions: Also known as first-class functions, these can be created at runtime, stored in data structures, passed as arguments to other functions, or used as a return value.

2.2. Transition from Imperative

In traditional programming, a program's state changes over time. An imperative approach also means that we write for-loops and while-loops that continually change the state of a variable until an outcome gets reached. However, functional programming uses recursion to repeat a sequence of operations, eliminating this variable mutation. Beginners might find recursion's concept somewhat daunting. However, it becomes more comfortable and intuitive to grasp as you get along.

FP might seem counter-intuitive if you are coming from an imperative programming background. But understanding why there's been a transition towards functional programming will shed light on its importance.

2.3. Why Functional Programming?

The shift towards functional programming is driven by an increasingly multicore and parallel computing environment. Debugging and reasoning become much more feasible when you don't have to worry about a program state that continually changes.

The principles like immutability eliminate problems like deadlocks, race conditions, and other situations that can crash a multicore program. With multithreading, multiple things are happening all at once, and it becomes tough to manage a system where variables can change at any moment.

The concepts of functional programming can help manage this

complexity. It enforces a much more disciplined approach to change, where functions depend only on the inputs provided and not on any hidden inputs or state.

2.4. Python and Functional Programming

While Python is not a 'functional programming language' in the purest sense, it does incorporate several functional programming features that allow for powerful and flexible coding. The one we're about to explore and delve deeper into is 'Lambda Functions'. But before we do, let's reinforce our understanding of what functions are in the context of Python.

2.5. Functions in Python

A function, in Python, is a block of reusable code that performs a specific task. Functions help break our program into smaller and modular chunks. As our program grows larger and more complex, functions make it more organized and manageable.

Furthermore, it avoids repetition and makes the code reusable. A Python function is defined using the def keyword. Functions need not always be named. If defined right in the place where you need to run a function, they're known as anonymous or Lambda functions.

In general, functionalities encapsulated into functions can be reused many times in a program. Python also allows function recursion, which means a defined function can call itself.

2.6. Lambda Functions: A Sneak Peek

Lambda functions are small, anonymous functions that are defined with the lambda keyword, hence the name. They can take any number of arguments but can have only one expression. While they visually look different than a standard Python function defined with def, they can be used anywhere function objects are required.

Lambda functions are a small and restrictive function kind. But this restriction - that only a single expression is allowed - is why they can be handy in many contexts where you need something that a function can do, but don't want to go to the trouble of defining a full function.

To demystify Lambda functions further and how they elevate your functional programming experience with Python, we'll delve deeper in the subsequent sections. But before we do, remember that understanding the function and functional programming principles are critical to harnessing their full potential. We hope this introduction has served to lay a solid foundation for you on your Python journey.

Chapter 3. Laying the Groundwork: Python's Functional Programming Tools

Python, being a versatile language, supports multiple programming paradigms, one of them being functional programming. Before we delve into Lambda Functions, let's explore some fundamental concepts and tools of functional programming in Python to lay a strong foundation.

3.1. Understanding Functional Programming

Functional programming is a programming paradigm where programs are constructed by applying and composing functions. It is built on the concept of 'pure functions', which, given the same inputs, always produce the same outputs. They neither depend on nor produce side effects. Python equips us with several tools to implement functional programming.

3.2. Pure Functions

A pure function is a deterministic function that always produces the same result for the same input and leaves the outside world unchanged. It operates solely on the input parameters, does not use or alter any global or instance variables, and does not have any side effect, like displaying a value or getting user input. Instead, it communicates with the world by returning a value. For example:

```python
def add(a, b):
    return a + b
```

In this example, `add` is a pure function. Given the same `a` and `b`, it will always return the same result, and it does not change anything in the world around it.

3.3. Built-In Functional Programming Tools

Python includes several built-in functions that follow the functional programming paradigm. These include, but aren't limited to `map()`, `reduce()`, `filter()`, `lambda`, and list comprehensions. These tools help you to write functional style code with ease.

3.4. Map Function

The `map()` function allows you to apply a function to every element in an iterable (like a list) without using any explicit loop. Here's how it works:

```python
numbers = [1, 2, 3, 4, 5]
squares = list(map(lambda x: x ** 2, numbers))
```

In the example above, `map()` applies a lambda function that squares a number to each item in the `numbers` list.

3.5. Filter Function

The `filter()` function allows you to filter elements in an iterable. It constructs a list from elements of an iterable for which a function returns true. Here's how you use this function:

```
numbers = [1, 2, 3, 4, 5]
evens = list(filter(lambda x: x % 2 == 0, numbers))
```

3.6. Reduce Function

The `reduce()` function, provided in the `functools` module, is a function that applies a binary function to an iterable in a cumulative way. For instance, if you need to find the product of all numbers in a list:

```
from functools import reduce

numbers = [1, 2, 3, 4, 5]
product = reduce((lambda x, y: x * y), numbers)
```

3.7. List Comprehensions

Python's list comprehensions are a prime example of Python supporting functional programming concepts. They provide a simplified way to create lists based on existing lists. For example, if we want to find the square of each number in a list, we could use a list comprehension:

```
numbers = [1, 2, 3, 4, 5]
squares = [x**2 for x in numbers]
```

3.8. Working with Higher-Order Functions

In functional programming, a higher-order function is a function that takes one or more functions as arguments, and/or produces a function as its result. Higher-order functions bring a lot of flexibility and opportunities for reusability and abstraction.

For instance, the `map()`, `filter()`, and `reduce()` functions are all higher-order functions since they take a function as an argument.

3.9. Immutability in Functional Programming

Immutability plays a crucial role in functional programming. An immutable object is an object whose state cannot be changed after it is created. Python has some built-in immutable types, such as strings, tuples, and namedtuples from the collections module.

This property brings several benefits, including consistency, readability, and ease of reasoning and debugging, while reducing the chances of introducing bugs.

Unearthing the power of functional programming in Python can be a game-changer in your coding journey. With these tools and concepts in hand, we are now ready to dive into the heart of Python's functional paradigm - Lambda Functions.

Chapter 4. Python Lambda Functions: The Anatomy of a Single Line Function

Functional programming is a paradigm that often mystifies those accustomed to the more common procedural paradigm. But there's one utility that can serve as a gentle — and incredibly useful — introduction: Lambda functions, also known as anonymous functions. As comfortable in a single-line statement as they are nested among Giants, Lambda functions are hugely adaptable, and can ease and speed up your coding process considerably.

4.1. Understanding Lambda Functions

Lambda functions, or "anonymous functions", are functions without a name. While normal functions are defined using the 'def' keyword, lambda functions are defined using 'lambda'. A lambda function can have any number of arguments, but it can only have one expression. That expression is evaluated and returned.

Lambda functions are utilized when you require a function for a short period of time and are generally used in situations where passing a function to another function is required.

A typical syntax of lambda function is:

```
x = lambda arguments : expression
```

This might seem a bit abstract, so let's break it down, piece by piece, to get a grasp of this special function:

4.2. The Lambda Keyword: Starting Point of a Lambda Function

The 'lambda' keyword is a token that declares the start of an anonymous function (not bound to any identifier). It's what separates ordinary functions from their nameless counterparts, prompting Python to expect a different type of syntax.

4.3. Arguments: Giving Inputs to Lambda Function

Following the 'lambda' keyword, you provide an argument list. A lambda function can accept zero or more arguments, comma-separated, just like regular functions. However, unlike traditional functions, you don't need to enclose these arguments in parentheses.

4.4. Colon: The Separator

A colon (:) separates the arguments from the expression within a lambda function. It's a component of Python's syntax rule that explicitly separates argument and expression fields.

4.5. Expression: The Functional Part of Lambda Function

The final part of a lambda function is the expression, which the function is bound to execute. A lambda function can have only one expression, which is evaluated and returned when the function is called. Try to keep the expression as simple as possible, because complex lambda functions can make your code less readable.

Now, let's see some lambda functions in action to better understand these principles.

4.6. Simple Lambda Functions

For instance, here's a simple lambda function that adds 10 to the number passed in as the argument:

```python
x = lambda a : a + 10
print(x(5)) # > 15
```

In the example above, the lambda function received the number 5 as its argument 'a'. After executing the expression (a + 10), the function returned the result (15).

Here is a lambda function with multiple arguments but still maintaining its one-liner charm:

```python
y = lambda a, b : a * b
print(y(5, 6)) # > 30
```

In the example above, the lambda function takes 5 and 6 as its arguments and returns the product of these inputs upon execution.

4.7. Why use Lambda Functions?

Lambda functions in Python have a number of notable utilities and advantages. Let's cover a few of these:

1. **Simplicity**: Lambda functions significantly simplify writing small functions.
2. **In-line declaring**: They offer an easy way to declare a function in a line and thus can inline small, throwaway functions at the place of their usage.

3. **Functional Coding**: Since they are anonymous (they have no name), they support good functional programming practices by promoting code that's more atomic, clear, and easy to understand.

4. **Higher-level operations**: Lambda functions work brilliantly with Python's functional programming modules like 'map()', 'filter()', and 'reduce()' which, often require function objects.

Lambda functions are not meant to be a wholesale replacement for 'def' defined functions. Instead, they are particularly useful when you need some functionality not more than once.

4.8. The Power of Lambda in Combination with Python's Built-ins

Built-in functions like 'map()', 'filter()', and 'reduce()' are perfect candidates for utilizing Lambda functions. These built-in functions are designed to apply any given function on iterable objects like lists, tuples, etc. We'll discuss how we can utilize lambda functions with these in the next chapters.

4.9. Lambda Functions vs Regular Functions

Lambda functions provide a concise way to create functions. However, while they can make code significantly cleaner when used in appropriate situations, they aren't a complete substitute for full function definitions. Their power lies in their simplicity and their single-use nature.

In closing, we can see that Lambda functions in Python are an incredibly powerful tool, given their flexibility and utility. Their ability to encapsulate functionality, operate on lists, and perform complex operations — all within a single, succinct line of code — makes them a critical resource to any Python programmer looking to leverage the full potential of the language.

Chapter 5. Power Unveiled: Understanding the Syntax and Structure of Lambda Functions

Understanding Lambda Functions start with its most basic element - the syntax and structure. At first glance, the form might seem a bit daunting, but it's relatively straightforward once examined piece by piece.

5.1. Introducing the Syntax of Lambda Functions

The fundamental form of a lambda function in Python is as follows:

```
lambda arguments : expression
```

Here, 'lambda' is a keyword, indicating the definition of an anonymous function. 'Arguments' represent the parameters the function will intake, and 'expression' is the functionality the lambda function will perform.

Remember - lambda functions can have any number of arguments but only one expression, which is evaluated and returned.

5.2. The Power behind the Seeming Simplicity

Although the syntax of the lambda appears simple, don't

underestimate its power. The lambda function's unique structure allows for flexibility and brevity, enabling you to create functions on-the-fly and keep your code clean and manageable.

Let's take a look at an example to solidify this concept. Below is an anonymous function that adds two numbers:

```
adder = lambda x, y: x + y
print(adder(1, 3))  # Output: 4
```

Here, x and y are the arguments, and the expression x + y returns the sum. We can assign this function to a variable (in our example, adder) to call it later on.

5.3. Dealing with Single and Multiple Parameters

Lambda functions are malleable and can accommodate a single parameter, multiple parameters, or even no parameters. When using multiple parameters, separate each parameter with a comma.

For instance, here's a lambda function example with a single argument:

```
square = lambda x: x*x
print(square(5))  # Output: 25
```

And another with multiple arguments:

```
multiply = lambda x, y: x*y
print(multiply(3, 4))  # Output: 12
```

Notice how the code remains clear and succinct. This defining characteristic of lambda functions encourages programmers to use them wisely.

5.4. Conditions inside Lambda Functions

Lambda functions are not limited to mathematical operations; they can incorporate logical conditions and return different outcomes based on these conditions. A closer look at this capacity uncovers the real strength behind Python's lambda functions: creating dynamic and powerful code constructs that can elegantly handle complex scenarios.

Below is an example of a lambda function using an 'if-else' condition:

```
greater = lambda x, y: x if x > y else y
print(greater(4, 5))  # Output: 5
```

Here, the function checks if x is greater than y. If true, it returns x; otherwise, it returns y.

5.5. Iterating with Lambda Functions

Lambda functions pair well with functions like map(), filter(), and reduce(). They help iterate over lists, allowing for computation on large datasets without the necessity for explicit loops, thus simplifying the code.

Consider the following example:

```python
numbers = [1, 2, 3, 4, 5]
squares = list(map(lambda x: x*x, numbers))
print(squares)  # Output: [1, 4, 9, 16, 25]
```

In this snippet, the `map()` function applies the lambda function to each element in the `numbers` list, resulting in the `squares` list.

5.6. The Trade-Offs

While lambda functions offer brevity and elegance, they aren't always the best choice. Their anonymous nature and single-line restriction can make the code less readable, especially for complex logic. As such, it's crucial to balance the use of lambda functions with other Python functions and constructs.

Understanding and using lambda functions is about more than just learning the syntax; it's about understanding the tool's strengths, limitations, and best use cases. This journey begins with syntax, but it elevates your functional programming potential when applied with discernment and strategy.

Lambda functions may seem slight in their form, but they are mighty in action. Learning to wield this tool effectively is like adding a powerful and versatile weapon to your arsenal of Python skills. The syntax and structure of lambdas might appear puzzling at first, but getting a grasp on these can unlock the key to efficient and streamlined program execution. Together with their ability to seamlessly pair with other Python constructs, lambda functions indeed pack a punch. Armed with this knowledge, you can truly leverage the power of functional programming in Python. Enjoy wielding this power!

Chapter 6. Mastering Expressions: Crafting and Using Lambda Expressions

Before diving into Python's Lambda Functions, understanding what lambda is, is a prerequisite. Derived from lambda calculus, a mathematical system introduced by Alonzo Church in the 1930s, the purpose of lambda calculus is to investigate function abstraction and application using variable binding and substitution. It explores functions without specifying the detail of the function body. Python's Lambda Functions borrow this concept, providing a way to declare small and anonymous functions.

Let's start coding now!

6.1. Anonymous(Lambda) Functions

In Python, lambda functions are small, anonymous functions that are declared with the keyword `lambda`, hence their name. The form of lambda functions in Python is: `lambda arguments: expression`.

```python
x = lambda a, b: a * b
print(x(5, 6))
```

In the above example, we have a function `x` that takes two arguments and returns their multiplication. When we call `x(5, 6)`, it returns `30`.

The ability to maintain such compact expressions gives Python an edge, allowing it not to limit itself to the definition of large functions. However, lambda is not just about making our programs shorter. It's also about improving their readability and efficiency.

6.2. Power of Lambda

Lambda functions can accept any number of arguments but must only have one expression. They cannot include complex logic or multiple expressions. They can be used wherever function objects are required and are syntactically restricted to a single expression.

The power of lambda can be better seen when you use them as an anonymous function inside another function. Let's consider a function that doubles the output of a function passed to it:

```python
def my_doubler(func):
    def wrapper(*args, **kwargs):
        return func(*args, **kwargs) * 2
    return wrapper


def summation(a, b):
    return a + b


result = my_doubler(summation)
print(result(5, 7))  # prints 24
```

In the above example, we have a helper function `my_doubler` that accepts a function and doubles the result of the function. It works, but we can make it more elegant with a lambda function:

```python
def my_doubler(func):
    return lambda *args, **kwargs: func(*args, **kwargs) * 2


result = my_doubler(lambda a, b: a + b)
print(result(5, 7))  # prints 24
```

Here we're passing a lambda function as an argument to `my_doubler`.

It not only shortens the code but also improves readability.

6.3. Lambda with Map, Reduce, and Filter

Lambda functions are incredibly potent when used in conjunction with Python's built-in functions such as map, reduce, and filter, which accept functionality as a parameter.

The map function applies a given function to each item of an iterable (e.g., list) and returns a list of the results.

```python
my_list = [1, 2, 3, 4, 5]
squared = list(map(lambda x: x**2, my_list))
print(squared)
```

When executed, this script prints [1, 4, 9, 16, 25].

filter creates a list of elements for which a function returns true. Here is a short and straightforward example:

```python
my_list = [1, 2, 3, 4, 5]
evens = list(filter(lambda x: x % 2 == 0, my_list))
print(evens)
```

When you run this script, it will print [2, 4], displaying only the even numbers.

Finally, reduce isn't a built-in function and must be imported from the functools module. It applies a rolling computation to sequential pairs of values in a list and returns a single result.

```python
from functools import reduce
```

```python
my_list = [1, 2, 3, 4, 5]
product = reduce((lambda x, y: x * y), my_list)
print(product)
```

This script prints `120`, which is the product of all numbers of `my_list`.

To sum up, Lambda Functions might look peculiar when you first encounter them, especially if you're still getting to grips with Python's syntax. However, once you get a hang of them, they can make your code much more readable and expressive. By mastering Lambda Functions, you can code more pythonically and leverage the full power of this versatile language. Happy Coding!

Chapter 7. Small Wonder: Strengthening Code with Lambda Functions

In the broad spectrum of Python programming, Lambda Functions are those unique, unadorned artists that shine through with simplicity, versatility, and efficacy. Despite their compact form, they pack an inordinate amount of power, enabling developers to tackle a wide array of programming tasks with ease and precision.

7.1. A Little History

Python adopted lambda functions from Lisp, one of the oldest high-level programming languages, primarily used for artificial intelligence research. In Lisp, lambda functions were synonymous with anonymous functions. This liberty to exist and operate without a formal name also extends to lambda functions in Python, a characteristic that lends them their distinctive ability to streamline code and empower programmers with the succinct expression.

7.2. The Essence of Lambda Functions

The lambda keyword in Python gives birth to anonymous functions, which follow the form: lambda arguments: expression. This can be an intimidating form when first encountered, but let's break down the syntax to help make it more understandable.

The keyword lambda is used to denote the start of the lambda function. Following it are the function arguments, defined in the same way as regular arguments in typical function definitions. After the colon comes the function expression. This expression is evaluated and returned when the function is called.

What makes lambda functions so powerful is their simplicity. They are stripped down and honed for singular purposes.

7.3. A Close Inspection of Lambda Syntax

Let's illustrate with a simple example. Suppose we want to create a function that adds two numbers. Here's the standard Python function:

```python
def add(x, y):
    return x + y
```

This seems pretty straightforward. But utilizing a lambda function, we can reduce it to a single line:

```python
add = lambda x, y: x + y
```

The two pieces of code perform the exact same operation, the difference simply being how the function is defined. This is the essence of lambda functions: the power of functionality embedded in simplicity and conciseness.

7.4. When to Use Lambda Functions?

Lambda functions shine their brightest in scenarios where brevity takes precedence, like when functions are used as arguments, or in conjunction with built-in functions such as map(), filter(), and reduce().

Let's consider an example wherein we want to multiply each element in a list by two:

```python
numbers = [1, 2, 3, 4, 5]
res = map(lambda x: x*2, numbers)
print(list(res))    # Output: [2, 4, 6, 8, 10]
```

In this example, the lambda function takes an argument x and returns x*2. This function is fed into the map() function along with the list of numbers. map() calls the provided lambda function on each element of the numbers list and returns a map object with the result, which we then convert back to a list to print.

7.5. Lambda with Filter

Filter, as its name suggests, is used to filter the content of a list (or any iterable) based on a criterion defined by a function. This function should return either True or False, and filter will use it to decide which elements to keep.

Here is a quick demonstration of how to use filter with a lambda function to filter out the even numbers in a list:

```python
numbers = [1, 2, 3, 4, 5]
res = filter(lambda x: x%2 == 0, numbers)
print(list(res))    # Output: [2, 4]
```

7.6. Lambda with Reduce

The reduce function comes from the functools module and it's used to reduce an iterable to a single output. It applies a binary function (a function with two arguments) to the elements of the iterable in a cumulative way. The first two elements are processed, and then the result is processed with the third one, and so on.

Here's an example where we use reduce, along with a lambda function to find the product of all numbers in a list:

```python
from functools import reduce

numbers = [1, 2, 3, 4, 5]
res = reduce(lambda x, y: x*y, numbers)
print(res)     # Output: 120
```

As demonstrated, the reducing process starts with the first two numbers (1*2) and their product is then multiplied by the next number (2*3), and so forth, until we get the final result (120).

7.7. Imperfections and Controversies

While lambda functions bring a lot to the table in terms of brevity and convenience, not everyone in the Python community is fond of them. Indeed, Guido van Rossum (Python's creator) considered removing lambda functions when developing Python 3.

The main reason is readability. Whereas short lambda functions can be easier to read due to their simpleness, this might not be the case when the complexity arises. Higher complexity can lead to less interpretable one-liners which can confuse other coders who are reading or maintaining the code. Notwithstanding this controversy, lambda functions still exist in Python, and when used judiciously, are a compelling tool in Python's repertoire.

7.8. Bringing It All Together

Lambda functions, simple yet powerful, are a cornerstone of functional programming paradigms in Python. They are versatile and flexible, allowing developers to write cleaner and more efficient code in a reduce-and-conquer manner, executing complicated tasks with a few heavy strokes. Despite their detractors, lambda functions are here to stay, and learning to harness these small wonders offers a valuable toolset for every Python programmer. Your journey through Python's functional landscape thus becomes more engaging and nuanced, empowering you to build more concise and effective solutions.

Chapter 8. Real-World Applications: Using Lambda Functions Effectively

Lambda functions, often called anonymous functions, are a unique feature of Python that allows us to perform quick, small-scale operations without the need of formally defining a function with def. They are one-tool armies capable of executing several tasks while maintaining the code's neatness and readability. With their growing popularity among Python enthusiasts, understanding how to use them in real-world applications is a crucial step towards coding proficiency.

8.1. Getting Started with Lambda Functions

Start by understanding the anatomy of a lambda function. It follows the syntax: `lambda arguments:expression`. Here, 'arguments' denote the parameters or inputs to the function, and 'expression' represents the operation we want to perform.

For instance,

```python
square = lambda x: x ** 2
print(square(4))
```

This code defines a lambda function that calculates the square of a given number. Easy to comprehend, isn't it? Now, let's delve deeper into these 'mysterious' lambda functions by dissecting their typical use-cases in real-world applications.

8.2. Data Manipulation with Lambda Functions

One of the most common use-cases of lambda functions is data manipulation within data-analysis libraries like pandas. Let us look at an example where we manipulate data in a pandas dataframe.

```python
import pandas as pd

data = {'Name':['Tom', 'Nick', 'John', 'Tom'],
'Age':[20, 21, 19, 20]}
df = pd.DataFrame(data)

df['Name'] = df['Name'].apply(lambda x: x.upper())
print(df)
```

In this example, we use a lambda function to convert each value in the 'Name' column to uppercase. Notice the 'apply()' function. It allows us to apply the lambda function to each row of the specified column. The lambda function turns out to be a cleaner and efficient alternative to defining and calling a proper function for such straightforward operations.

8.3. Sorting Collections With Lambda Functions

Lambda functions can also shine while sorting collections. Let us consider a list of tuples, where each tuple represents a person's name and age.

```python
people = [('John', 20), ('Ana', 22), ('Mark', 21),
('Lisa', 23)]
```

```
people.sort(key=lambda x:x[1])
print(people)
```

Here, we sort the list of tuples based on the age (the second element of the tuple), using a lambda function passed to the 'key' parameter of the 'sort()' method. As a result, we acquire a sorted list of tuples in ascending order of ages.

8.4. Lambda Functions in Functional Programming

Functional programming concepts, particularly 'filter()', 'map()', and 'reduce()', pair exceptionally well with lambda functions. Let's demonstrate this via real-world-inspired examples.

Chapter 9. Filtering Data

The 'filter()' function filters the given iterable with the help of a function that tests each element in the input for being true or not.

```
numbers = [10, 21, 30, 33, 40, 51]
odd_numbers = list(filter(lambda x: x % 2 != 0,
numbers))
print(odd_numbers)
```

In this case, we use a lambda function to filter the list to have only odd numbers.

Chapter 10. Map Function

The 'map()' function applies a given function to all items in an input list.

```python
numbers = [1, 2, 3, 4, 5]
squares = list(map(lambda x: x ** 2, numbers))
print(squares)
```

Here, we use a lambda function to calculate the squares of all numbers in the list.

Chapter 11. Reduce Function

The 'reduce()' function applies a rolling computation to sequential pairs of values in a list.

```python
from functools import reduce

numbers = [1, 2, 3, 4, 5]
product = reduce((lambda x, y: x * y), numbers)
print(product)
```

In this example, we calculate the product of all elements in the list using the 'reduce' function.

11.1. Lambda Handlers in AWS

Lambda functions in Python are widely used for serverless operations in AWS (Amazon Web Services). They serve as a key component, referred to as Lambda Handlers. A Lambda Handler is a Python script that runs in response to an AWS event.

```python
def lambda_handler(event, context):
    # ...event handling code
    return
```

Although this is not strictly a 'lambda' function in Python terms, it borrows its philosophy in the sense that it is an anonymous function triggered by an event.

In conclusion, Python's Lambda functions, while perplexing for newcomers, are powerful, flexible coding tools when used appropriately. Their effective handling can help you write more concise, readable code for various real-world applications—be it data manipulation, sorting collections, working with other functional constructs, or designing serverless operations under AWS. Embrace the power of Lambda, and watch your productivity and code efficiency elevate tremendously.

Chapter 12. Lambda in Action: Practical Examples and Case Studies

With the basic theory established, it's time to delve into the practical application of Lambda Functions. In this extensive section, we'll explore and dissect numerous practical examples and case studies showcasing the functionality and versatility of Python Lambda Functions.

12.1. The Basics Brush-up: Lambda

Writing a lambda function is relatively straightforward. A lambda function is an anonymous function declared with lambda keyword, followed by variables, a colon and the expression. Here's an example:

```
adder = lambda x, y: x + y
print(adder(5, 3))
```

This will output 8. Here we have a function adder which takes in two arguments and returns their sum.

Lambda functions come in handy owing to their one-time usage and disposability, making our code cleaner and more efficient.

12.2. Using Lambdas with Python Built-in Functions

Many Python built-ins accept functions as arguments. Lambda functions shine when used with these built-ins. Two such functions, "filter()" and "map()," stand out in highlighting lambdas' utility.

Use of lambdas with `filter()`:

The `filter()` function takes a function and a list as arguments. This function offers a convenient way to filter out elements from any sequence. For example, to filter out all even numbers from a list, you would do so:

```python
numbers = [1, 2, 3, 4, 5, 6]
even_numbers = list(filter(lambda x: x % 2 == 0,
numbers))
print(even_numbers)
```

Resulting output would be: `[2, 4, 6]`.

Utilizing lambdas with `map()`:

Similar to `filter()`, the `map()` function takes a function and a list as arguments, applying the function to each item of the iterable. To double every item in a list:

```python
numbers = [1, 2, 3, 4, 5]
doubled = list(map(lambda x: x * 2, numbers))
print(doubled)
```

What you get is: `[2, 4, 6, 8, 10]`.

Can you see how lambdas synergize with Python's powerful built-in functions for simpler yet efficient operations?

12.3. Lambdas with List Comprehensions

Let's advance our mastering of lambdas by combining two distinct Python features, namely Lambda Functions and List Comprehensions.

```python
numbers = [1, 2, 3, 4, 5]
squared = [(lambda x: x ** 2)(x) for x in numbers]
print(squared)
```

The output of the above code will be: [1, 4, 9, 16, 25].

This tiny piece of elegant code goes a long way to prove the charm of combining lambda functions with list comprehensions.

12.4. Higher Order Functions

Higher-order functions refer to functions that: take one or more functions as arguments, and/or return a function as its result.

Lambdas serve as brilliant tools when paired with higher-order functions. For instance, to sort a list of strings by length:

```python
words = ["Python", "is", "easy", "to", "learn"]
words.sort(key=lambda s: len(s))
print(words)
```

The output would show the words sorted by their lengths: ['is', 'to', 'easy', 'Python', 'learn'].

We passed a lambda to the sort() function's key parameter, allowing us to sort the strings by their length.

12.5. The Art of Nesting Lambdas

Although not a common practice, understanding how to nest Lambda Functions can sometimes come in handy for complex problems.

```python
# a simple lambda function
adder = lambda x: lambda y: x + y
print(adder(5)(3))
```

The output will be 8. This multilevel nesting, often abstract, may appear daunting, but once mastered, it brings unparalleled depth and dynamism to your Python arsenal.

As we wrap up this explorative section, it is evident that Lambda Functions exhibit a unique mix of simplicity, flexibility, and power, making them a vital part of any Python programmer's toolkit. Whether it's a quick one-time function to use with `filter()` or `map()`, or a higher-order function accepting a lambda as its parameter, understanding lambdas will empower you to write more efficient, cleaner and more Pythonic code. Almost like unseen heroes, Python lambda functions help enhance code readability while minimizing unnecessary code lines, effects that become particularly pronounced in larger, more complex coding projects.

Chapter 13. Pairing Lambda with Built-Ins: Map, Filter, Reduce and More

Python's Lambda functions embody a crucial facet of functional programming, assisting in code optimization by offering compact, reusable solutions for myriad programming challenges. One area where lambda functions stand out is their interoperability with built-in Python functions like map(), filter(), and reduce(). These combined yield formidable power capable of simplifying even the most complex tasks. Here, we unfold the mysteries of these fascinating synergies.

13.1. Utilizing Lambda with Map Function

Python's map() function is a powerful tool that applies a given function to each element in an iterable. When combined with lambda, map() allows for significant code optimization. The standard structure for using map() along with lambda is:

```
map(lambda x: x * 2, iterable)
```

[/PYTHON CODE]

In this structure, "x" is the argument to the lambda function, and "x * 2" represents what the function should return for each iterable element. The iterable can be any Python iterable object, such as lists or tuples.

Let's illustrate this with an example. Say you have a list of five numbers, and you want to square each. Binding map() with a lambda function would look like this:

```python
numbers = [2, 1, 3, 4, 5]
result = map(lambda x: x ** 2, numbers)
print(list(result))  # Prints: [4, 1, 9, 16, 25]
```

[/PYTHON CODE]

In this code, "lambda x: x ** 2" is a function that takes "x" and returns its square. map() applies this function to every item in "numbers", and the result is returned as a map object.

13.2. Pairing Lambda with Filter Function

The filter() function in Python extracts elements from an iterable for which a function returns True. Combining lambda functions with filter() provides robust filtering capabilities without extra lines of code for custom functions.

The typical structure for using filter() alongside lambda looks like this:

```python
filter(lambda x: (x%2 == 0), iterable)
```

[/PYTHON CODE]

In this construct, "x" is the lambda function's argument, and "x%2 == 0" determines if the function will return True or False for each item in the iterable.

For illustration, assume you have a list of numbers and want to filter out the even ones. Here's how you can utilize lambda with filter():

```python
numbers = [2, 1, 3, 4, 5, 6, 7, 8, 9]
filtered_result = filter(lambda x: (x%2 == 0), numbers)
print(list(filtered_result))  # Prints: [2, 4, 6, 8]
```

[/PYTHON CODE]

This code cleverly applies the lambda function to filter out odd numbers, leaving only even ones in the final result.

13.3. Combining Lambda with Reduce Function

Python's reduce() function is part of the functools module and functions differently from map() and filter(). reduce() continually applies a function to a sequence of elements, effectively reducing the sequence to a single output.

The standard structure for using reduce() with lambda would be:

```python
from functools import reduce
reduce(lambda x, y: x*y, iterable)
```

[/PYTHON CODE]

For instance, calculate the product of all the numbers in a list with reduce() and lambda:

```python
from functools import reduce
numbers = [1, 2, 3, 4, 5]
product = reduce(lambda x, y: x*y, numbers)
```

```
    print(product)  # Prints: 120
```

[/PYTHON CODE]

In this example, the lambda function takes two arguments, x and y, and multiplies them. reduce() applies this operation across the entire list, producing the total product of all elements.

13.4. Leveraging Lambda Functions with Other Built-ins

Beyond map(), filter(), and reduce(), Python nurtures a suite of built-in functions that can be further empowered by lambda functions — 'sorted()' serves as an example. By default, 'sorted()' sorts an iterable based on standard comparisons. However, you can designate a lambda function as the key parameter to forge custom sorting mechanisms.

For example, sort a list of tuples based on the second value of each tuple:

```
data = [("John", 55), ("Anna", 22), ("George", 67),
("Sophia", 33)]
sorted_result = sorted(data, key=lambda x: x[1])
print(sorted_result)
# Prints: [('Anna', 22), ('Sophia', 33), ('John', 55),
('George', 67)]
```

[/PYTHON CODE]

In the above code, a lambda function forms the key to compare each tuple during the sorting process. The lambda function receives 'x' as a tuple from the 'data' list and returns 'x[1]', i.e., the second element. Consequently, the 'sorted()' function reorders the tuples based on this key.

Through the presented examples, we radiate how integrating lambda functions with Python's built-ins like map(), filter(), and reduce() advances your functional programming skills. This blend enables tighter and more efficient code while preserving clarity, making it a potent tool for every Python programmer's arsenal. As with every powerful instrument, efficient use comes with practice. Therefore, challenge yourself — write more code, solve more problems, and continually bridge your knowledge gaps. Happy Coding!

Chapter 14. Riding the Wave: The Future of Lambda Functions in Python and Beyond

The pages of the Python history book are studded with numerous transformative features, and one equally enigmatic yet critical is Lambda Functions. They're much more than an advantageous, alternative syntax; Lambda Functions portend an expansive, exciting future, destined to redefine Python programming in the years to come.

14.1. The Versatility of Lambda

Lambda Functions' adaptability to changing scenarios underpins its expansive potential. Python, as a language, is witnessing an exponential growth in developing both, scripting-based and data-heavy applications. As data manipulation needs surge, so ascend the demands for compact, efficient, and reusable coding structures, and Lambda Functions perfectly fit the bill.

Considering some immediate examples, one cannot ignore the role of Lambda Functions in data science libraries like pandas, with its `.apply()` or `.map()` functions, regularly utilizing Lambda Functions for on-the-fly calculations. Similarly, sorting complex data structures has been simplified using Lambda Functions in conjunction with the `sorted()` method.

14.2. The Streamlined Design

The design and implementation of Lambda Functions appropriately suits the simplicity ethos of Python. As Python progresses towards further simplification and readability in syntax, the addition of more functional programming features, perhaps even Lambda Functions with more than one expression, could come to the fore on the Python coding landscape.

Simultaneously, more hybrid programming approaches could witness incorporation or expansion of Lambda Functions. The world of concurrent programming could see the rise of Lambda Functions as parallel code execution, and task-Lambda Function pairings become increasingly common.

14.3. The Growing Ecosystem

The Python ecosystem's continuous growth is an important aspect to consider when analyzing Lambda Functions' future. New packages and modules are frequently launched to cater to varying programming needs. Alongside, the existing popular libraries evolve, driving adoption of esoteric Lambda functionality in an array of fields, from data science to web development, from computational mathematics to scripts automation.

Moreover, the Python community's diligent steerage gears the language towards greater efficiency. The increased adoption of Lambda Functions for coding contests and hackathons are testament to this trend. Such occasions could witness the birth of creative, unprecedented implementations of Lambda Functions that could eventually become standard practices.

14.4. Lambda Influence on Learning Curves

As Lambda Functions become mainstream, we might witness a shift in the Python learning curve. Traditionally, Lambda Functions are introduced quite late in Python tutorials, often labeled as an "advanced" concept. However, their expansive usage might necessitate early introduction, right alongside functions or modules.

On a global scale, this would mean a change in pedagogical approach, making students comfortable with functional programming alongside object-oriented and procedural styles. This approach won't just augment coding versatility but also pave the path for more innovative uses of Lambda Functions.

14.5. Python and Beyond

Interestingly, Python isn't solely driving the leap in Lambda Functions adoption. Other programming languages, like JavaScript, are also propelling the lambda wave with anonymous or unnamed functions. Hence, inter-language learning and adoption are likely phenomena in the future, with Python borrowing best practices from other languages and vice versa.

Witnessing this trend, Python may expand the current abilities of its Lambda Functions or import some features from other languages while retaining the core simplification ethos. This cross-pollination of ideas across languages can significantly elevate Python's coding standard and its relationship with Lambda Functions.

14.6. Final Thoughts

Lambda Functions signify the forward wave of Python programming. Locked within this concept is the potential to redefine coding styles, transform data manipulation, and dictate future Python versions. As lambda rolls further into mainstream, Python itself evolves, promising exciting new horizons, and reinforcing the reputation of Python as an adaptable, efficient, and dynamic language.

Experts, novice programmers, and everyone in-between should ramp up their Lambda Functions understanding and usage as part of their continuous learning process. Not only do they symbolize the future of Python, but they're an integral part of the ever-evolving programming realm whose possibilities are as expansive as our collective coding imagination.

Change might spawn challenges, but as Lambda Functions reshape Python's contours, they inherently promise an exhilarating journey - a journey all Python programmers ought to embark on, prepped with the nuances of Lambda Functions, ready to ride the wave of the future.